My Poetry Speaks

Monique Renee Trotter

BALBOA.PRESS

A DIVISION OF HAY HOUSE

Balboa Press books may be ordered through booksellers or by contacting:

Balboa Press
A Division of Hay House
1663 Liberty Drive
Bloomington, IN 47403
www.balboapress.com
844-682-1282

Print information available on the last page.

ISBN: 978-1-9822-7736-9 (sc)
ISBN: 978-1-9822-7737-6 (e)

Balboa Press rev. date: 11/10/2021

Contents

A Kiss to Geri Martindale

A pretty picture is just a pretty picture
But a loyal heart makes a true friend
You bless the world with your genius love
And your genius love brings hearts to the world
A simple smile will always do
And you have such a lovely smile
I want to touch you with my words
A rose that is greater than grand
Will always bloom in the midst of December
Your love is never doubting me...the sweetest love of all
My wings shall fly to the top of the mountain
Your poetry dares me to dream
I am happy because you are my friend
The roses in the garden have so much potential
But not as much as you
Your words are willing to go the distance
But mine is silent rage
I love you for the human that you are
A crystal chandelier that shines bright in the light
Your skin is glowing
And your eyes are swimming in the ocean
I cannot wait to meet you someday.

Be My Valentine

I can't believe I love you
More than the eyes can see
Romantically I am involved
But in my dreams, I am forever with you
Sunny days and blue skies are beyond hearts and flowers
I want you in my life no matter what
Bells ring, can we get married now?
My vast resilience shall set me free
For my truelove must understand
Oh, Valentine be dear to me
I am helplessly in a trance
You are a man of great stature, beauty, and grace
My breath feels your breath
Two breaths make life complete
Cupid's arrow is never broken
When love is in the air
Birds fly but they never cry
So high in the sky
I am reaching out to you,
Are you reaching out to me?
Thoughts of a destined love letter occur.

The Miracle of Cupid

Love's wings do grow eternally
I shall die a lonely soul
For I can't breathe through open air,
I am a twisted sparrow
My saddest days are gifted
Each bird that flies has a twinkle in his eye
My harrowing fate shall put me at ease
Yet a gifted mind shall never retire
My hands are tied to this here place
Exercising the right to love unconditionally
The very best of mourning has gone to sea
My feelings are weak in heart's spring
Oh passionate butterfly do not run,
Do not bother to sail away
For he has bestowed upon me now
The greatest gift of love
Matters of the heart seem to be a little baffled
This endless war between you and I
Breaking the silence that is Cupid
A bird with a spoken arrow
Speaks louder than anything I have ever seen
So let it be known that love is in the air
Risking its days and lonely nights
The poor and shallow ones begin to follow
The strange creature that is me.

Dead Flowers in the Stream

I want to be left alone with you tonight
I want my woes to be found
A poisonous snake lies within a broken heart
For silence is a deadly sound
Beware of the fake poets that have no rhythm
A sunless garden cannot bear its shame
For poetry lives within the hearts of true poets
I must shun you with my decorum
In the beam of light
There is a strong effervescence
The life we live is forsaken
I want to appear mad, but not deeply frightened
Sorrowful eyes begin to rise
The naked truth has captured its essence
The flowers are in denial
There is no water left in the stream
I dare not live to see another day
Unless my love feels for me.

The Ocean Breathes Salty

My life is not so reassured
The very deepest of my regrets
Yet I own what is left of me
The spiritual box that still stands
The higher desire to fix what is broken
I can't leave these riddles unsolved
Hopefully you will remember me when the time comes
Well you say love exists
Well I don't know what to believe
The sun finds me guilty
But truth be told
The lies just keep getting bigger
I have one hand to hold,
And that hand is mine
Swimming in the darkness that is pure
The rage inside this lonely beast
Opens many dreams to be expected
I play the silent game alone
An angel in white dances as she passes by
My holy truth is not a truth that will set me free
Though many things have been lost and gone
Of trial and error
The ocean is very deep
I find it to be my greatest release
The circumstances of a thousand ships
Resign perfectly.

Roses in the Fire

Your heart is a beautiful cloud
Floating upon dreams
As ashes fall from the sky
You make every dream worthwhile
I feel so pretty
I feel so free
I want to dance in the wind
That carries the fire within
My joy is everlasting
Love is a burning flame
Between the ashes
You give to me
A dozen roses
Therefore you shall live
Forever in my memory.

Reasonable Doubt

If my soul is free
How can I breathe?
My mind trembles
And my eyes do see
I am destined for greatness
Yet what is love?
White pillows and white sheets
Suffocating into the blue
I am a little girl dressed in roses
Behold the inside of an open door
Life is beautiful with trees and everything
The tears that fall from heaven's cloud
I dare not speak out loud
If beauty haunts me
Then I shall surrender
To the greatness that is me
Long lives the fire that dies inside
The flame that opens a broken window
I shouldn't question life and all of its resentments
I shouldn't question the sparks in the sky
A forbidden romance between us both
The thunderous passion that lies.

Old Friends

The mystery that solves everything is still in tact
The magnetic eagle that sings
Though all is holy through the month of November
The wild eyes that lie
A dozen roses fall from earth
Goodbye forever
I will forever miss you
The distance between us shall remain
Through butterflies and chains
Our hearts will someday heal
No more stupid games
And dreams will forever raise these clouds
Above the endless skies
So here is a rose for you
And here is a rose for me
Let us remember what we had
For those very few moments in time
Old friend.

Roses Are Red

This is straight from the heart
If roses are blue, then what are you?
There is an open gate at the end of heaven
Every breath you breathe shall be my last breath
Falling endlessly to tears
So if roses are red, then what am I?
The music that speaks to me fades
I love you
Kill me with your sorrow
For the tears are an ocean at the end of every corner
A red rose for every drop of blood...yes my heart bleeds
Beautifully haunting is the soul
My thoughts unwind
A rose for every rose
A heart for every heart
A taste of freedom that dies
I've been living without you for quite sometime
And you know I can't live without you
Where is this rose that makes your heart beat?
Am I still alive?
Unlock the key that locks your heart
I want to be able to stand
For every rose that has your heart
Is not as red as mine.

Extraordinary Love

You know I'm really feeling you
The things that go on inside my head
I'm constantly thinking of you
My heart bleeds fair, oh this fair bleeding heart
I want no other love
Take me vastly in your arms
Before the whole world begins to fall apart
In the blink of a lover's eye
There's no hope for tomorrow
For we are living in the moment
A moment that will last forever
The breath of a rose will always live deep inside
The enigma that is you will die
There shall be no more clouds in the sky
As memories linger on like yesterday's news
I'm not here to swallow any tears
Though loving you can be such a helpless crime
Yes I am guilty, guilty of loving you
Until you give me a reason not to love again
The world is full of passion
For we are living in a passionate world
I shall chase my shadow in the wind
For my spirit is free
I want to be with my shadow
My shadow in the wind.

To My Everlasting Valentine

You are an everlasting thought
My lips quiver to your soft demands
In fantasies that have yet to be fulfilled
I am one lucky rose
That belongs to one lucky man
The magic is in the mystery
And I am lost in your magic
You are a breath of fresh air
In the midst of falling in love
I hold on to every word you speak
As sparks fly like birds in the sky
I am so happy to be alive
You are much sweeter than fifty chocolate kisses
In a heart-shaped box
And every poem is the sweetest poem ever written
Love...is there any other four-letter word
That makes one's heart explode?
The sun is always brighter on Valentine's Day
Whether or not I'm embracing the moment alone
Which leads me to believe
Love is the key to all eternity.
As fragile as the day is long
My heart sings a song
A song that shall dance
Whenever you think of me.

Killing Me Softly

I'm sitting here listening to our song
A song so reminiscent
I'm constantly thinking of you
It's not fair
You're in my head
And I see you everywhere
I'm too shy to ever speak to you again
But not too shy to write what I'm feeling
Still, I have a soft spot in my heart for you
Emotions run deep
You make me laugh
You make me cry
Sometimes you rock my world
Yeah we had a moment or two
When we made love so hard it hurt
Pain is love
Love is pain.

Infectious

Your lovely words
Shivering down my spine
I'm alive, yes I'm alive
Lips quivering
As temptation enters
Hot and bothered
Late at night
Your soft kisses
Your careless whisper
Our bodies in motion
Like a restless tide
Heavy breathing
Breathing heavy
Let's go down
All the way down
Until the sun rises
Then we come back up
Up for air
Sunshine upon our faces
As we lie
In each other's arms
Exhausted.

Private Obsession

I am deeply in love with you
For lust is the greatest sin
What fool am I
And I shall be a fool until the day I die
As I behold the infinite amount of stars in the sky
Heaven is a pretty awesome view
For it is your twinkling eye that captures me so
I can't imagine anything more perfect
The passion is endless when I am at peace
Fondly touching my emotions
The wooing of the wind is such sweet song
I hearken at your command
Ha, what shall become of this spirited affair?
A veil of mystery lingers in the air
Lost lovers indeed escaping from reality
The night is young and so are we.

The Relapse

You make me surrender
With the deepest of passion
I don't have to lie to tell the truth
Yes I am afraid of commitment
Only because I can't endure it
Though it seems you know how to reach me
Maybe someday you will understand
How I feel about you exactly
We get through hard times
Like they're just ordinary days
You are my heart, my soul, my tears
You are a magnetic high that reaches no bounds
As long as I'm breathing
Normally I live my life in a solitary bubble
Nothing exciting ever happens to me in there
I just feed off my insatiable words
That make somewhat decent poetry
Between the lines and between the sheets
Red rose petals are never too sweet
You kiss me as if I'm a complete stranger
And that's perfectly alright with me
The skies smell like perfume
And the clouds taste like cotton candy
You touch me and I feel the heavens ignite.

One Sweet Wind

I'm missing you again
My heart surrenders every time you call my name
You give me great fever
When you hold me up to the sky
The magic in the moment never dies
Even if it's just for a little while
With twelve tender kisses
You have me sighing
Ah the world is a beautiful place
Whenever you're around
The sun sings and the clouds dance
As my imagination runs wild
You make me triumphant,
You make me unique
The power of poetry seems to put all the pieces together
Still I'm missing you again
Come back to me sweet wind
Your love is as sweet as a newborn child
At last, at last my words are dear
To something so rare and debonair
One sweet wind, one sweet dream
One sweet melody
That will carry me for all eternity.

Vast Enlightenment

Counting every star
Is not as grand as wishing upon a lonely star
When the spirit moves me, I feel I am alive
The universe dares me to spread my wings and fly
This is not my last chance to shine
As my journey continues
I will find my destiny
Or will my destiny find me?
In the spirit of angels
I shall prosper with everything I am worth
I am the sea
I am the sky
I am the mountain way up high
As my words dance across the page once again
For my one and only love
That lonely star shining upon me
Somewhere out there in the world
Ah two lonely souls make a perfect one
A perfect one for all the other stars to see
Oh I'm longing, longing to marry that lonely star
My mind is completely blown
Vast enlightenment, vast enlightenment
I am here to follow you
Oh my heart is so fragile and sweet
Every day is a whole new experience
Yet you are still a beautiful stranger to me
A mystery in the making.

Enchanted Feelings

I fear the essence of time
Will wrap itself around my hips
And take away my righteous dignity
I am a woman
Full-blown to my extent
Talk dirty to me
But don't use any four-letter words
I challenge you to undress me
With just your eyes
What do you see?
And why do you see it?
Beauty is not based upon dreams
The world is as tender as a T-bone steak
Wrapped in the gods of men
I am amused with the undertaker
Medium rare but not yet raw.

To The Man Behind the Smile

As I light a candle in the wind
The music starts to play
Whenever you appear in my wholehearted dreams
The sky is vast and sleeping sound
A gentle kiss whispers the sound of your voice
The words just fly like simple birds
For sound is the greatest thing that ever lived
Within the hopes and dreams of poets
Your eyes have failed to blind me now
You look at me as if I am weary
The blankets cover my half naked silhouette
Let us elope into the fire
Breathing the life of such bliss
Your heroic love shall strive for goodness
You and I shall have our last fight
Between oceans of endless light
For eternity is endless
And so is the love
I am not coming home
I want to stay in the moment with you
Light my key in the spirit of love
Ah the death of a rose is only temporary
Whisper again your deep southern voice
Let me hear the words that make me yearn
For I shall fly like a simple bird.

A Simple Twist of Fate

I am so pretty
I can fly without wings
I can stay in one perfect place
Roses thrill me with delight
Because the world seems so peaceful
And tomorrow will be a brilliant day
Time pushes bounds to single limits
My skin is pale and my eyes are brown
I feel your beauty all around me
I love the way your dark hair shines
Beneath the sun that is cold and dear
No one will ever understand
The person we've come to be
There is a tree outside your window
And I am standing ten feet tall
Yes I hear the wind dancing beneath me
As you touch the leaves so bare
I dream of the perfect song,
The perfect song that is you
Those lips that speak so eloquently
The fire in those eyes
Poetry is a part of every living being
Those who can't feel are already dead inside.

A Rose in The Sky

I know I'm too complicated to understand
But someday I will tell you how beautiful you are
Well heaven is a remarkable circumstance
My knees begin to crumble
And my heart begins to wonder why
I am not a human flute
I am a human emotion
Floating around in the depths of October
The sun has no words
The moon is dancing in the wind
Behold the loudest reason of all
Fire sprouting like wild grass
See how I am skin and bones
And you are a perfect rose
A rose so pink without the thorns
See how your petals grow
Right in front of your foolish eyes
I can't let you go
My memory won't let me
As pink ribbons fly among the trees
Long yet everlasting
Is the life that lives above the clouds
Sing to me oh foolish one
Sing to me your darling praise.

Love and Stars

I cannot love without a star
And you are the star of the show
My darling Kewayne,
A rose with a brilliant name
I shall honor you
Beyond the kiss of poetry lies
A deeper sense of connection
I must continue to be inspired
Your lovely light shines through
Sweet heaven fills the earth
There's no end in sight
One love, one star, one burning flame
Has reached a higher power
Someday I shall be as grand as you
A rocket exploding into millions of stars
May you live to be an immortal poet
In a world where I am sane
My darling Kewayne,
A rose with a flourishing pen
I shall honor you.

Beast Of Rapture

Ah the rarities of love
Filled with magic and despair
I can only hope the causes are deep
Yet rendering till the living end
Give me a tender praise of warning
As the lights go out.

About the Author

Monique Trotter is an aspiring poet who dreams of being well known and loved by many. She started writing at the age of seven, but back then writing was just a hobby. She didn't know how powerful her writings were until she was told by others that she had a gift. Later on, Monique Trotter entered many poetry contests and won several awards. She also went to a few conventions and met other fascinating poets. Writing is her passion, and this is something she wants to continue for the rest of her life. Monique believes poetry fulfills the soul and ignites the heart. Ladies and gentleman, here is the next famous poet.

Printed in the United States
by Baker & Taylor Publisher Services